The No-Cook, Skinny, Nutritious, Oat Smoothies Cookbook

Marjorie Kramer

2014

Disclaimer

 Understand that the information contained in this book is an opinion, and should be used for personal entertainment purposes only. You are responsible for your own behavior, and this book is not to be considered medical, legal, or personal advice. Nor is this book to be understood as putting forth any cure for any type of acute or chronic health problems or psychological illness. The programs and information expressed within this book are not medical advice, but rather represent the author's opinions and are solely for informational and educational purposes. The author and publisher is not responsible in any manner whatsoever for any injury or health condition that may occur through following the programs and opinions expressed herein. Dietary information is presented for informational purposes only and may not be appropriate for all individuals.

Consult with your physician before starting any rigorous exercise program or altering your diet.

Books by Marjorie Kramer

1. The No-Cook, Skinny, Delicious, Nutritious Overnight Oats in a Jar Cookbook
2. The No-Cook, Skinny, Delicious, Nutritious, Oat Smoothies Cookbook
3. The 4 Ingredients Paleo Cookbook – All The Recipes Have 4 Ingredients or Fewer!
4. The 2 Ingredient Cookbook – All The Recipes Have Only 2 Ingredients!
5. The 2 Ingredient Dessert Cookbook – All the recipes have only 2 ingredients!
6. The 26 Worst Facebook Grammar Mistakes Ever & How to Avoid Them
7. Charting New Territory in ESL – What You Wish Your ESL Book Included

Table of Contents

Disclaimer	2
Books by Marjorie Kramer	4
Introduction	7
Apple Pie Oat Smoothie	12
Beet and Berry Oat Smoothie	13
Blueberries and Cream Oat Smoothie	14
Blueberry Banana Oat Smoothie	15
Cherry and Peach Oat Smoothie	16
Chocolate Almond Oat Smoothie	17
Chocolate Chip Oat Cookie Smoothie	18
Mixed Berry Oat Smoothie	20
Oatmeal Cookie Dough Smoothie	21
Oatmeal Cookie Smoothie	22
Oatmeal Raisin Smoothie	23
Orange Creamsicle Oat Smoothie	24
Peach Oat Smoothie	25
Pear Ginger Cinnamon Oat Smoothie	26
Peanut Butter Banana Oat Smoothie	27
Pineapple Oat Smoothie	28

Purple Berry Oat Smoothie	29
Raspberry Oat Smoothie	30
Simple Strawberry Oat Smoothie	31
Strawberry Pecan Oat Smoothie	32
Review	34

Introduction

This is the sister book to **The No-Cook, Skinny, Delicious, Nutritious, Overnight Oats in a Jar Cookbook.** In that book, I discuss how to make Overnight Oats in a Jar and why they're so good for you. Here, I'm going to supply you with some equally as delicious and nutritious **SMOOTHIE** recipes for those mornings when you wake up with a desire to drink, rather than eat, your breakfast. Some of these smoothies stay in the fridge overnight like the Overnight Oats recipes, and some you can eat right away.

A big part of a skinny, healthful diet plan is a skinny, healthful breakfast. These fantastic, no-cook "Oat Smoothies" breakfasts are nourishing, crammed with fiber, vitamins, protein, and calcium, and are low in fat and sugar. Their popularity, like that of "overnight oats in a jar," is growing like wildfire. Now that summer is upon us, the "no cooking" aspect of these breakfast stars is adding to their fame. Did I mention how to make them? You dump the few ingredients into your blender, blend everything up, and stick it in the fridge!

That's it! Next morning – breakfast is served! You can even freeze them (leave 3/4" at the top of the container), so that you have breakfast made for a week in advance! What the heck else could you ask for?

Let's run back over some of the information about these easy, great breakfasts.

There is a huge amount of evidence that eating raw oats every morning can, with the help of regular exercise, significantly lower high cholesterol. The oats will also keep you regular, help your metabolism, keep you from getting hungry between meals, and help maintain the health of your liver, skin, nervous system, and red blood cells. We recommend the old-fashioned rolled oats over other types because they are less processed, and therefore better for you. You can prepare and use oats in your smoothies in different ways, all of which are suggested within the recipes. Some folks think the thing to do is to grind them up in your blender before you add the other ingredients. Others like to use the oats whole and let them soften (often with chia seeds) in the fridge for a few hours to a couple days. You can play with them in these recipes and decide which ways you prefer.

Chia seeds are incredibly good for you. Among other qualities, they have more Omega 3 than flax seed, help maintain hydration, help with weight loss, have as much protein as quinoa, and are high in calcium, Vitamin B, and antioxidants. They are eaten whole, have a two-year shelf life, and will take on the flavor of other ingredients in a recipe. That's one mighty seed! One thing you need to do when blending oats and/or chia seeds dry is use a long-handled spoon to get either or both up from the bottom when you add the liquid. Without doing that, they could get stuck at the bottom.

The difference between Greek yogurt and "regular" yogurt is that the Greek has been strained to take out whey. This makes Greek have 40% less sugar, less sodium, and twice the protein of its cousin. Another health facet helped by Greek yogurt is your digestion, aided by the yogurt's probiotic content. Greek yogurt also helps in lowering blood pressure. Its high protein content helps with weight management, and its nutrients aid in building strong bones.

For sweeteners, I like Stevia. Stevia is natural, has a negligible effect on blood glucose, and causes no insulin spike when ingested. This means it's great for diabetics and for hypoglycemics like me. Stevia tastes exactly like sugar to me. However, I have heard that other people can get a bitter aftertaste from it. I've also heard that NuNaturals liquid Stevia might be the fix for that. Other sweetener choices are honey, maple syrup, dark or light brown sugar, sucanat, and turbinado or "raw" sugar. You can, of course, use white sugar, but why would you when there are so many better options?

Use the ripe fruit of your choice. Some fruit may do better if you leave the Overnight Oats in the fridge longer than overnight. Bananas are definitely best with one night only.

If you want to freeze your smoothie (great idea; breakfasts ready for a week!) first place them in the fridge for at least four hours to let them soak. Then you can put them in the freezer. To defrost, transfer the smoothie from freezer to fridge the day before.

Now that you know all about Oat Smoothies, let's get to the recipes!

Apple Pie Oat Smoothie

Ingredients

1/3 cup old-fashioned rolled oats, uncooked

1 large apple of any type

1 cup milk of your choice

1 tsp Honey

1 tsp Cinnamon

1/2 c. ice

Directions

Quarter the apple.

Take out all of the core. (Your choice of leaving the peel on or not.)

Put all ingredients into the blender.

Blend all together.

Adjust for thickness and sweetness.

Put into fridge for at least four hours.

Blend again.

Beet and Berry Oat Smoothie

Ingredients

1/2 cup old-fashioned rolled oats, uncooked

1 Tbsp chia seeds

1 small beet, raw or cooked

a large handful of red grapes

10 frozen strawberries

few frozen raspberries and blueberries

Directions

Pulse oats and chia seeds a few times in your blender.

Put all ingredients into the blender.

Blend all together.

Adjust for thickness and sweetness.

Put into fridge for at least four hours.

Blend again.

Blueberries and Cream Oat Smoothie

Ingredients

1/2 cup old-fashioned rolled oats, uncooked

3/4 cup frozen blueberries

1/2 cup frozen banana slices

1/2 cup loosely packed spinach

1/2 cup plain Greek yogurt

2 pitted dates

1 cup almond milk

Directions

Put all ingredients into your blender.

Blend until smooth.

Put into fridge for at least four hours.

Blueberry Banana Oat Smoothie

Ingredients

1/3 heaping cup old-fashioned rolled oats, uncooked

3/4 cup vanilla almond milk

1 honey-flavored Greek yogurt

1/4 cup blueberries

1 large frozen banana

3 frozen strawberries

Directions

Put the first four ingredients into bowl. Stir.

Cover and put in the fridge overnight.

Put this mixture into the blender.

Add the frozen banana and strawberries.

Blend until smooth.

Top with granola, coconut, seeds or nuts.

Cherry and Peach Oat Smoothie

Ingredients

1/2 c. old-fashioned rolled oats, uncooked

1-1/2 tsp chia seeds

1 c. any kind of milk or juice

1 c. Greek yogurt

1 c. cherries and peaches

2 Tbsp honey or your favorite sweetener, or 1 - 2 Tbsp jam

1/8 tsp cinnamon (optional)

Directions

Put all ingredients into the blender.

Blend all together.

Adjust for thickness and sweetness.

Put into fridge for at least four hours.

Blend again.

Chocolate Almond Oat Smoothie

Ingredients

1/2 c. old-fashioned rolled oats, uncooked

1 large frozen banana

2 Tbsp unsweetened cacao powder

2 Tbsp almond butter

1 c. spinach

1 tsp vanilla extract

5 dates, pitted and diced

1/2 tsp ground cinnamon

1/4 tsp ground nutmeg

2 c. almond milk

Directions

Put all ingredients into the blender.

Blend all together.

Adjust for thickness and sweetness.

Put into fridge for at least four hours.

Blend again.

Chocolate Chip Oat Cookie Smoothie

Ingredients

1/2 cup old-fashioned rolled oats, uncooked

1 Tbsp chia seeds

1 1/4 – 1 3/4 c. unsweetened almond milk, divided

1 small frozen banana

3 medjool dates, pitted or add your favorite sweetener, to taste

2 Tbsp almond butter

2 Tbsp raw cacao nibs, or dark chocolate chips

1 tsp raw cacao powder, or unsweetened cocoa powder

1/2 tsp pure vanilla extract

1/8 tsp almond extract or vanilla extract

handful of ice

Directions

Blend together 3/4 cup milk, the oats, and the chia seeds.

Put into fridge for at least four hours.

Add all the other ingredients, beginning with 1/2 cup milk.

Blend all together.

Adjust for thickness and sweetness.

Blend again.

Mixed Berry Oat Smoothie

Ingredients

1/2 c. old-fashioned oats, uncooked

1 Tbsp chia seed

1 c. almond milk

1/3 c. fresh squeeze orange juice

1 frozen banana

2 c. frozen mixed berries, including cherries

2 c. spinach

1 Tbsp matchi powder(optional)

1/2 c. Greek yogurt

1/4 c. walnuts

Directions

Put all ingredients into your blender.

Blend all together.

Adjust for thickness and sweetness.

Put into fridge for at least four hours.

Blend again.

Oatmeal Cookie Dough Smoothie

Ingredients

1/4 c. old-fashioned rolled oats, uncooked

1 small frozen banana

1 tsp chia seeds

1/2 - 1 scoop vanilla protein powder

1/2 tsp cinnamon

1 tsp vanilla extract

1 Tbsp almond butter

1/2 cup your choice of milk

Directions

Put all of the ingredients into your blender and mix well.

Serve immediately or put it into the fridge for a couple hours.

Oatmeal Cookie Smoothie

Ingredients

1/4 c. old-fashioned rolled oats, uncooked

1 frozen (peeled) banana

1 c. unsweetened almond milk

1 - 2 Tbsp honey (to taste)

1/2 tsp ground cinnamon

1/2 tsp vanilla extract

1/4 tsp ground ginger

pinch of nutmeg

pinch of salt

(optional: 1/4 cup raisins)

Directions

Pulse oats and chia seeds a few times in your blender.

Add the rest of the ingredients.

Blend all together.

Adjust for thickness and sweetness.

Serve immediately, or put into fridge for a couple hours.

Blend again.

Oatmeal Raisin Smoothie

Ingredients

4 Tbsp old-fashioned rolled oats, uncooked

1/2 c. your choice of milk

1/2 c. plain Greek yogurt

1/2 banana

1 oz raisins

1 tsp brown sugar

1/2 tsp vanilla

1/4 tsp ground cinnamon

2 c. ice

Directions

Put all the ingredients, except the ice, into your blender.

Blend until smooth.

Add the ice.

Blend again, moving the ice into the mixture with a long-handled spoon.

Serve immediately, or put into the fridge for a couple hours.

Orange Creamsicle Oat Smoothie

Ingredients

1/2 c. old-fashioned rolled oats, uncooked

1T chia seeds

1 c. almond/coconut milk

1/2 c. peach

1/2 c. mango

1/2 carrot

splash of OJ.

Directions

Put all ingredients into the blender.

Blend all together.

Adjust for thickness and sweetness.

Put into fridge for at least four hours.

Blend again.

Peach Oat Smoothie

Ingredients

1/4 c. old-fashioned rolled oats, uncooked

1 Tbsp chia seeds

1/2 c. almond milk

1/4 c. fresh orange juice

2 ripe peaches, with pits removed and quartered

1/2 frozen banana (peeled before freezing)

a bit of the sweetener of your choice

Directions

Put all ingredients into the blender.

Blend all together.

Adjust for thickness and sweetness.

Put into fridge for at least four hours.

Blend again.

Pear Ginger Cinnamon Oat Smoothie

Ingredients

1/4 c. old-fashioned rolled oats, uncooked

1 cup frozen, diced pear

1/2 tsp grated ginger

1/2 tsp cinnamon

1/2 c. plain, nonfat Greek yogurt

3/4 c. milk

1 Tbsp honey

Directions

Put all ingredients into the blender.

Blend all together.

Adjust for thickness and sweetness.

Serve immediately or put into fridge for a couple hours.

Blend again.

Peanut Butter Banana Oat Smoothie

Ingredients

1 c. old-fashioned rolled oats, uncooked

2 bananas

1 c. any kind of milk

1 c. vanilla yogurt

1/4 c. natural peanut butter

1 tsp cinnamon

2 - 3 large scoops ice or more

Directions

Put all ingredients into the blender.

Blend all together.

Adjust for thickness and sweetness.

Put into fridge for at least four hours.

Blend again.

Pineapple Oat Smoothie

Ingredients

1/4 c. old-fashioned rolled oats, uncooked

1 c. frozen pineapple

1/2 c. ice cubes

1 packet stevia

Ground cinnamon, to taste

1 c. water

Directions

Put the oats in the blender, and pulse until they are powder.

With blender off, add the water.

Add the rest of the ingredients and blend.

Serve immediately or put in the fridge for a couple hours.

Blend again.

Purple Berry Oat Smoothie

Ingredients

1/2 c. old-fashioned rolled oats, uncooked

1 Tbsp chia seeds

1 c. almond/coconut milk

frozen banana

frozen blueberries

frozen strawberries

a splash of OJ.

Directions

Put all ingredients into the blender.

Blend all together.

Adjust for thickness and sweetness.

Put into fridge for at least four hours.

Blend again.

Raspberry Oat Smoothie

Ingredients

1/4 c. old-fashioned rolled oats, uncooked

1 banana

1 c. frozen red raspberries

1 container (6 oz) Yoplait Original French Vanilla Yogurt

1/2 c. cold water

1/4 c. coconut milk

1/4 tsp vanilla

Directions

Put all ingredients into the blender.

Blend all together.

Adjust for thickness and sweetness.

You can serve immediately or put it into fridge for a couple hours.

Blend again.

Simple Strawberry Oat Smoothie

Ingredients

1/2 c. old-fashioned rolled oats, uncooked

1 Tbsp chia seeds

1 c. frozen, sliced strawberries, or about 12 - 14 whole strawberries

1/2 c. frozen banana slices

1/2 tsp vanilla extract

1 c. almond milk or 1 cup vanilla yogurt

2 - 3 pitted dates or sweetener of your choice

Directions

Put all ingredients into your blender.

Blend all together.

Adjust for thickness and sweetness.

Put into fridge for at least four hours.

Blend again.

Strawberry Pecan Oat Smoothie

Ingredients

1/4 c. old-fashioned rolled oats, uncooked

1 1/2 tsp chia seeds

1 c. milk of your choice

1/4 c. vanilla Greek yogurt

1 c. strawberries, sliced

1 Tbsp pecans, ground, or nut butter of your choice

1/4 tsp cinnamon

1/2 tsp vanilla bean paste or extract

scoop of vanilla protein powder (optional)

sweetener of your choice

Directions

Add the oats and the chia seeds to your blender.

Blend on high until it's a powder.

Put all other ingredients except sweetener into the blender.

Blend all together.

Stir up the from the bottom to ensure that the oat mixture gets mixed in.

Adjust for thickness and sweetness.

Blend again.

Put into fridge for at least four hours.

Blend again.

Review

I hope you've enjoyed this book of recipes of Oat Smoothies. Please check out its sister book, *The No-Cook, Skinny, Delicious, Nutritious Overnight Oats in a Jar Cookbook*!

Enjoy this book?

Please leave a review, and let us know what you liked about this book.

Books by Marjorie Kramer

1. The No-Cook, Skinny, Delicious, Nutritious Overnight Oats in a Jar Cookbook
2. The No-Cook, Skinny, Delicious, Nutritious, Oat Smoothies Cookbook
3. The 4 Ingredients Paleo Cookbook – All The Recipes Have 4 Ingredients or Fewer!
4. The 2 Ingredient Cookbook – All The Recipes Have Only 2 Ingredients!
5. The 2 Ingredient Dessert Cookbook – All the recipes have only 2 ingredients!
6. The 26 Worst Facebook Grammar Mistakes Ever & How to Avoid Them
7. Charting New Territory in ESL – What You Wish Your ESL Book Included

Printed in Great Britain
by Amazon

39556302R00020